DR. SHELLY CAMERON

Author of Green Light

MY SAFE PLACE

YOUR REFUGE IN
TIMES OF TROUBLE

ISBN: 978-0-578-66532-0

Dr. Cameron, Shelly

www.shellycameron.com

First Printing 2021

Printed in United States of America

Dedicated to Kylie

And to those who are Afraid

For you are my hiding place;
you protect me from harm.

Psalm 32:7

GREENLIGHT

If you have not already done so, read the book **"GreenLight: When God Says Go."** It is available in paperback, kindle, and audiobook. These formats make it easy to access. GreenLight is about finding out the will of the Lord. We cannot get green lights before we are on the road. At the lights, we are told what to do. When we get to life's intersections, whether it is decision-making, career, business, or relationships, He tells us what to do. GreenLight has inspirational short stories and exhortations to uplift you, prayers for difficult journeys, and devotions to boost your prayer life.

What People are Saying *"Beautiful short stories which are so meaningful to life."*

Get your copy today.

CONTENTS

Introduction

At three in the morning, I received the most devastating news. My daughter's Godmother had lost her 15-year-old granddaughter; she had died of a massive Asthma attack. I screamed—quietly. I asked the Lord why, why, why? I did not understand. As I sought answers, her aunt encouraged that she did not understand either, but she was safe in the Lord's loving arms.

It brought back memories of when my uncle Carl had died suddenly. His passing led to my mom suffering a massive stroke that she succumbed to months later. If that were not enough, my brother died tragically within 24 hours of my mom's passing. What a year that was! I felt numb.

So what do you do when tragedy strikes? Where do you run? Where is your safe place? A quick search online came with answers, including libraries, YMCAs, fire stations and more. These places are intended to provide immediate help and support for people in need.

So, where is your safe place? One mom disclosed that her bedroom was her safe space for her two boys after her divorce. Some find solace in their home, job, finances, children, spouse, or family. When tragedy strikes, we run to a place where we feel safe. A place where we feel protected. A place that assures us that all will be well. Personally, my safe place is with the Lord. I love my family, but my safe place is with God. I am closest to him in the serenity of the beach where the sea flows, the birds fly and trees sway nearby. There are no surprises with him because he makes all things well.

Why This Book

This book was written as a sequel to its original, *GreenLight: When God Says Go*. It follows the theme of sharing inspirational short stories, poems, and exhortations to uplift you on your journey and relationship with the Lord.

The title "*My Safe Place*" arose when I was going through a period of change in my consulting work with a client. I was asked to assist with the implementation of an initiative. After completion, I was asked to help with a few other projects, to which I reluctantly but respectfully agreed. Months later, as I watched changes unfold, I kept my commitment to the organization. However, with little notice, the client rescinded.

I felt betrayed, saddened by a world where commitment to agreements mean nothing. In my disappointment, I ran to the Lord and he gave me the comforting words that my safe place was with him. That is when the stillness of my heart led to this writing.

Furthermore, as I finished the manuscript, I concluded that I did not have anyone to dedicate the book to as I had in my previous books which were based on my research of success, leadership, and motivation. Those were dedicated to my girls because I wanted them to be influenced by the same values to go after their dreams. However, immediately on learning the sad news, I knew that this book would be dedicated to

15-year-old Kylie, who died unexpectedly. Initially, I was confused. Why did the Lord let her die then brought her short life to this book? But as I pondered, I realized it was because her brief life meant so much to her loved ones and schoolmates. After all, she was a member of the yearbook club and was widely known for her soft smile and encouraging heart. Her death led others to Christ. So I know as well as her family, that she was born for that purpose. To stand up for the under-represented and for those who were afraid. So you see, it clicked. She is safe in his place—in His loving arms. May this book inspire you to go to Him as the spirit leads.

How To Read This Book

Within the contents of this book, I share a few of my experiences and those of others I have encountered. Readers can expect to glide through comfort, encouragement, confusion, what to do when making decisions, where to find peace and more.

Read a few at a time or a day at a time. The goal is to help you stay close to the Lord when the going gets rough and you become afraid and just want to run to a safe place. I hope you are inspired to curl up with him not only during the tough seasons but during those times of joy.

Blessings overflow.

*Write it down because I want
the faithful to be encouraged*

Habakkuk 2:2

MY SAFE PLACE IS WITH YOU

My safe place is with you Lord.

My safe place is with you.

When I am alone with you, I know all will be well.

But though my human heart cries out in pain,

showering the agony and pangs of defeat.

I cry out to you because you are the God who brings comfort.

You bring peace;

You bring solace.

My safe place is with you Lord;

My safe place is with you.

*Cast your cares on the Lord and he will sustain you;
he will never let the righteous be shaken.*

(Psalm 55:22)

WHEN GOD SAYS GO

HOW DOES GOD GET OUR ATTENTION?

God gets our attention in many ways. Dr. Charles Stanley shared several. God gets our attention through Restlessness. We have that Restless feeling that no matter what we do, there is no satisfaction. We still feel that prodding. There is no resolve until he gets our attention.

He Speaks Through Others. Sometimes he speaks through others. Be mindful of this as not everyone who gives you a word may be from him. So be wise. Stay in tune with his word and you will know when he speaks.

Through His Blessings. He blesses us and we are surprised. Have you ever received an unexpected gift that knocks you off your feet? It is as though it blows your mind, especially when you did not ask him but needed it. Then you start rejoicing and thanking Him.

When We Reflect On His Goodness. When we stop to think how good He is to us. When we reflect on what is happening around us, we look back at our past experiences and we cannot help but wonder how good he has been.

When He Answers our Prayers, God gets our attention through times of introspection and prayers when we ask, seek, and wait on him. He initiates and we give in to his prodding.

Through Disappointments. When we experience disappointments, we reflect to find out what He is saying to us.

Through Failure. Dr. Charles Stanley said, "Failure drives us to God." It might be the loss of a job, financial problems such as the loss of income, house, job opportunities or more. To avoid uneasy feelings, we try to help ourselves, but that hardly ever works. If it does work, often the solution is only temporary. Then we run back to him.

Through Sickness. Sometimes God wants something for us that we do not want for ourselves. Often, He wants more for us. Sometimes better. He wants the best. He wants us to walk in His steps. When we do, we will get His joy, support, acceptance, and is divine energy.

As you reflect on these points, are you getting that feeling that the Lord is trying to get your attention? Listen and respond today and avoid long periods of delay. In the end, His prodding leads to lasting satisfaction and peace.

You will weep no more. How gracious he will be when you cry for help! As soon as he hears, he will answer you. (Isiah 30:19)

LAUNCH OUT INTO THE DEEP

At various intervals in my life, I have heard messages from the Lord to Launch out into the deep. The story surrounds Jesus telling Simon Peter to launch out into the deep and let down his net to catch fish. The challenge? The fishermen had worked hard all night and there was no fish. However, when Peter obeyed, he had to call for help because of the catch. Their nets were so full that the nets began to tear.

The takeaway? At intervals in our lives, the Lord tells us to obey him and go where he sends us. Then He will make his plans for us real. We gain success when we obey him.

*When he had finished speaking, he said to Simon,
"Put out into deep water, and let down the nets for a
catch. Simon answered, "Master, we've worked hard
all night and haven't caught anything. But because
you say so, I will let down the nets." When they had
done so, they caught such a large number of fish that
their nets began to break. (Luke 5:4-6)*

FOR THE FIRST TIME

Mid-life she decided to move to Paris. A dream she always had. With kids grown and little or no responsibilities, she decided to take the plunge! She bought a house and exclaimed, "it's my first time." Instinctively I thought about that.

Personally, I have had many first times. An explorer and lover of adventure, I sky-dived for the first time. I moved to different states and countries for the first time. Oh and let me not forget my first time writing and publishing my research on Success Strategies. That book has helped many others for their first time.

I remember the first time I experienced childbirth. It was an exhilarating yet a humbling experience. Fourteen years later, I did it again for the first time and the experience was no different. Wonders of the world a little me was born again for the first time.

These days I reflect on the many first-time experiences that the Lord has been using to help me in my spiritual growth.

How about you? Is there something that the Lord has been prompting you to do but because it is your first time, you are afraid? Why not take the risk? Try it. Step out in faith. The Lord has everything under control and with him, you will always achieve his purpose when you walk in his will.

Go. Do what He has called you to do.

*So be careful to do what the Lord your God has
commanded you; do not turn aside to the right or to
the left. Walk in obedience to all that the Lord your
God has commanded you, so that you may live and
prosper and prolong your days in the land that you
will possess.*

(Deuteronomy 5:32-33)

I'M TOO OLD

I'm too old for a new career,

I'm too old for changing what they say,

I'm too old for finding sweet love,

I'm too old for my dreams to come through,

I'm too old;

I'm just too old.

Silly…

You're never too old to live your dreams;

You're never too old to change your life.

You're never too old to go after your heart's desire;

You're never too old to do anything you want.

You're never too old.

Never. Ever. Too Old.

*He gives power to the faint, and to him who has no
might he increases strength.*

(Isiah 40:29)

PSALM 31

In thee, O Lord, do I put my trust; let me never be ashamed:
deliver me in thy righteousness.
Bow down thine ear to me; deliver me speedily:
be thou my strong rock, for an house of defense to save me.
For thou art my rock and my fortress;
therefore for thy name's sake lead me, and guide me.
Pull me out of the net that they have laid privily for me:
for thou art my strength.
Into thine hand I commit my spirit:
thou hast redeemed me, O Lord God of truth.
I have hated them that regard lying vanities:
but I trust in the Lord.
I will be glad and rejoice in thy mercy:
for thou hast considered my trouble;
thou hast known my soul in adversities;
and hast not shut me up into the hand of the enemy:
thou hast set my feet in a large room.

Have mercy upon me, O Lord, for I am in trouble:
mine eye is consumed with grief, yea, my soul and my belly.
For my life is spent with grief, and my years with sighing:
my strength faileth because of mine iniquity,
and my bones are consumed.
I was a reproach among all mine enemies,
but especially among my neighbours, and a fear to mine
acquaintance:
they that did see me without fled from me.
I am forgotten as a dead man out of mind:
I am like a broken vessel.
For I have heard the slander of many: fear was on every side:
while they took counsel together against me,
they devised to take away my life.

But I trusted in thee, O Lord:
I said, Thou art my God.
My times are in thy hand:
deliver me from the hand of mine enemies,
and from them that persecute me.
Make thy face to shine upon thy servant:
save me for thy mercies' sake.
Let me not be ashamed, O Lord; for I have called upon thee:
let the wicked be ashamed, and let them be silent in the grave.
Let the lying lips be put to silence;
which speak grievous things proudly and contemptuously
against the righteous.

Oh how great is thy goodness,
which thou hast laid up for them that fear thee;
which thou hast wrought for them that trust in thee before the
sons of men!
Thou shalt hide them in the secret of thy presence from the
pride of man:
thou shalt keep them secretly in a pavilion from the strife of
tongues.
Blessed be the Lord:
for he hath shewed me his marvellous kindness in a strong city.
For I said in my haste, I am cut off from before thine eyes:
nevertheless thou heardest the voice of my supplications
when I cried unto thee.

O love the Lord, all ye his saints:
for the Lord preserveth the faithful,
and plentifully rewardeth the proud doer.
Be of good courage, and he shall strengthen your heart,
all ye that hope in the Lord.

GOD'S PURPOSE

NOT EVERY OPPORTUNITY IS FOR YOU

Years ago, I stepped out of my comfort zone. Having not been in the job market for a long time, I began my search for a new and meaningful opportunity. With great elation, a dream company reached out to me. It was always a goal to work with them. It had a great salary, great benefits, and most important – meaningful work. But I would have had to relocate—no problem for me as I did not have a chick nor child (as the saying goes…hint kid in college). I could hardly wait to get started.

A senior-level position, I had to go through a 5-level-interview process with different senior-level teams and nailed the toughest two. Then the onto the third. Nailed it! Or so I thought. The interviewer thought otherwise. They replied, thanking me for my time, but they decided to move on. After being interviewed for almost a month, I was confident and sure to get the job with my qualifications and experience. I did not. Though an interviewer myself, I was disappointed. I questioned myself—what did I do wrong? How could I have done better?

Not Every Opportunity Is for You

Then came the reassurance from a quiet inner voice. Not every opportunity is for you. What seems ideal may not be for you. Keep looking. The right change is in store. Learn to wait. And while you are waiting, trust him and remain strong.

Do not be anxious about anything, but in everything by prayer and supplication with thanksgiving let your requests be made known to God. And the peace of God, which surpasses all understanding, will guard your hearts and your minds in Christ Jesus (Philippians 4:6-7)

Closed Doors

Closed doors offer many opportunities for us to learn. Often, we are disappointed with delays as we seek the Lord's help in prayer to meet the needs and desires of our heart. May we gain the strength to wait to follow His lead. Dr. Charles Stanley encouraged that God can use our desires to teach us his ways. The Lord does it to mold us into His image; to prevent mistakes; to redirect our walk with him; to test our faith; to build perseverance as well as to buy us time.

At times, we fail to learn because of our impatience. Then later, we find that we were not ready for the opportunity. So today, I encourage you to remember that God's ways are not our ways, but he knows best. I encourage you to always trust him and seek his guidance.

Rejoice in hope, be patient in tribulation, be constant in prayer. (Romans 12:12)

I Don't Have Any Gifts

I overheard a discussion between two ladies in the salon as they were listening to the song "bless the Lord oh my soul… oh my soul, worship his holy name."

A little child was singing it, hence the reflection on 'gifts.' It caused me to think about the gifts God provides to us. One lady commented, "all I do is talk, gab a lot." I thought quietly—that is in fact, a gift. She can use her gift of 'gab' to become a speaker even in a small group. She can use her gift of 'gab' to write a book, to share positive thoughts with others. Personally, I believe there is enough negativity in the world.

So discover Your Gift. There are many assessments available in the marketplace to help you find your gift. These come in the form of leadership, encouragement, administration, faith, intercession, discernment, helping, teaching and more.

Many quietly wish for the gift of singing, dancing and entertaining because those gifts are quite popular. They can easily be seen and celebrated by others. But that was not the goal the Lord intended for us. The intent was for us to use our individual gifts to edify others.

Do you know that the more popular spiritual gifts often need support? Let us take, for example, singing. Singers sing but benefit from the gifts of songwriters. Movie-stars act but also need a script. Musicians play but need musical instruments designed and the list goes on.

Be assured that we need each other to soar in our different roles. That is how the Lord designed it. What you are is God's gift to you. What you become is your gift to God.

Now go, find your gift.

Every good gift and every perfect gift is from above, coming down from the Father of lights with whom there is no variation or shadow due to change.
(James 1:17)

The Street Life

Life is like walking the streets. No matter the street we are on, we should Walk by Faith. No matter the shoes we are wearing—new, old, running, stylish, high heels, low heels, wedges—we should walk by faith. Opportunities abound. Stepping forward, stepping out, taking the risk is well worth it. So find your street and achieve the dream the Lord planted in your spirit today.

But I say, walk by the Spirit, and you will not gratify the desires of the flesh. (Galations 5:16)

God Has A Purpose for Everything

My daughter's 8-year-old son prayed that a cure would be found for the Corona Virus. But each time he prayed, he ended with the words "unless you have a purpose Lord."

With my mouth aghast when I heard it the first time during the worldwide pandemic, I asked him to clarify. He said maybe God wants to bring us together or something. I knew then that he did understand.

I pray that we, too, will be like a child—simply trusting God for His sole purpose and plan. Together let us keep the faith when we do not know God's plan and purpose for what we are going through. Trust him.

Be patient, therefore, brothers, until the coming of the Lord. See how the farmer waits for the precious fruit of the earth, being patient about it, until it receives the early and the late rains. You also, be patient. (James 5:7-8)

PSALM 139

You have searched me, Lord,
and you know me.
You know when I sit and when I rise;
you perceive my thoughts from afar.
You discern my going out and my lying down;
you are familiar with all my ways.
Before a word is on my tongue
you, Lord, know it completely.
You hem me in behind and before,
and you lay your hand upon me.
Such knowledge is too wonderful for me,
too lofty for me to attain.

Where can I go from your Spirit?
Where can I flee from your presence?
If I go up to the heavens, you are there;
if I make my bed in the depths, you are there.
If I rise on the wings of the dawn,
if I settle on the far side of the sea,
even there your hand will guide me,
your right hand will hold me fast.
If I say, "Surely the darkness will hide me
and the light become night around me,"
even the darkness will not be dark to you;
the night will shine like the day,
for darkness is as light to you.

For you created my inmost being;
you knit me together in my mother's womb.
I praise you because I am fearfully and wonderfully made;
your works are wonderful,
I know that full well.

My frame was not hidden from you
when I was made in the secret place,
when I was woven together in the depths of the earth.
Your eyes saw my unformed body;
all the days ordained for me were written in your book
before one of them came to be.
How precious to me are your thoughts,[a] God!
How vast is the sum of them!
Were I to count them,
they would outnumber the grains of sand—
when I awake, I am still with you.

If only you, God, would slay the wicked!
Away from me, you who are bloodthirsty!
They speak of you with evil intent;
your adversaries misuse your name.
Do I not hate those who hate you, Lord,
and abhor those who are in rebellion against you?
I have nothing but hatred for them;
I count them my enemies.
Search me, God, and know my heart;
test me and know my anxious thoughts.
See if there is any offensive way in me,
and lead me in the way everlasting.

GOD'S GUIDANCE AND LEADING

When Goals Differ

I was driving behind a car when the traffic light changed yellow. It was more than enough time for the car ahead to go through. But the man behind the wheel purposefully slowed down to stop. Naturally, I was annoyed.

As I looked at him, I realized his goal was to stop to smoke. Mine was to get to work on time; it drove me crazy. He was chilling. I was late. He appeared to have gone to the gym and was unhurriedly getting back. I needed to go to the gym but cannot (smirk). He may have a job that he can go to when he pleases. Mine was to get there early, or else.

But though I hated his actions, he was living his choice. I must live with mine. We must stick with the choices we make.

On a deeper note, what choice have you made towards a deeper relationship with the Lord? Have you given that much thought? If not, why not choose to make that your goal? He will help you if only you call on him today.

Therefore the Lord waits to be gracious to you, and therefore he exalts himself to show mercy to you. For the Lord is a God of justice; blessed are all those who wait for him. (Isiah 30:18)

Face your Giant

What is going on in your life that seems like a giant? Is it a career decision? A conflict on the job? A conflict at home with your spouse, kids or loved ones? When you ponder your future, does it look bleak? If so, be confident that it does not have to be.

Fight the Good Fight. Often, we hide our pain. We brush it under carpets. We smile when deep down, we are hurting. Today be encouraged. Step out despite your fear or tear. Dig deep inside your soul and you will find the strength that you need to fight the good fight, to face what lies ahead—to conquer your giant by faith.

The Lord, He has got you.

Have I not commanded you? Be strong and courageous. Do not be terrified; do not be discouraged, for the Lord your God will be with you wherever you go. (Joshua 1:9)

How Can You Hear If You are Not Listening?

We are not reading the word. So how are we going to hear what He is saying to us? How are we going to get His guidance? His direction? How are we going to follow his leading?

We pray, plead and become sad. Our dreams, goals and aspirations seem stalled. We complain and ask questions.

Why?

Why aren't our prayers being answered?

Why the delay?

Why do we need to wait?

Why? Why? Why?

The Answer

Why worry when we can pray? Seek His word, read it and chew on it. In time you will glean His direction. Do not give up. Stay the course. He has you in the palm of his hands.

It is to be with him, and he is to read it all the days of his life so that he may learn to revere the Lord his God and follow carefully all the words of this law and these decrees. (Deuteronomy 17:19)

Examine Your Path

As is the tradition when approaching the end of a year, we are encouraged to reflect on the past year and plan for the new. Personally, I publish my annual year in review on my blog. It helps me celebrate achievements, recognize failures, setbacks and create plans for the ensuing year.

2020 was no different. Like me, many others made plans. Companies made corporate goals weaved into Strategic Plans. But then early in the year, the worldwide pandemic struck and we were all in disarray. What would we do? Where can we turn? Government mandates forced everyone to stay home and to stay safe. It was okay the first month. Then the second. By the third month, many were going crazy. We have to get out! Social media shared things people were doing to keep themselves encouraged. Laughter, cheer, styles, home renovations and more. Then suddenly, as we stepped into the fourth month, movements began, and people questioned whether society would ever find a vaccine or a cure.

But as the second half of the year progressed into the third Quarter, the hopeful decided to deepen prayers that the Lord would lead, guide, and direct their path. That said, check your plans. Are you where you wanted to be? If not, find your 'what and why,' then with God's help, create it because there is no future without God.

Examine your path. Look closely. You will see where he is leading.

May all that you do be done through his strength and according to his will and purpose for your life.

*The heart of man plans his way, but the Lord
establishes his steps. (Proverbs 16:9)*

The Bible In The Age of Technology

Sitting next to me in church, 10-year-old RJ whispered (Bible in hand), "nobody brings their Bible to church anymore." Then he told me to look around. He was right. I did not have my Bible in hand as Pastor Darryl read the displayed verses on the screen. Mine was resting quietly in my bag. RJ proceeded to draw a cartoon comic discussion about the missing Bible at church.

No excuses, but in the Technological era we now live in, most of us use the Bible App as our scripture reading resource. Convenience at its core, it is easy to carry around because we always have it on our phones. It is also easy to share a verse or two to encourage others who cross our minds while reading.

But at times, if there is no Wi-Fi, we can experience connection issues if we did not download the App in advance. Also, there is the risk we may end up scrolling to alerts that pop up if we are not strong and disciplined enough to avoid distractions. Nevertheless, I love the convenience of the App.

But yep! I agree with RJ. Very few actually carry the Bible anymore. But then let us not be quick to judge as we rejoice in the convenience it brings while at work, on the move anytime, anyplace. Join me in this simple challenge to take the physical book with you to church. Even more so, let us read our Bible and pray every day.

Blessings overflow to you as you listen while he speaks through the word. It ignites.

This Book of the Law shall not depart from your mouth, but you shall meditate on it day and night, so that you may be careful to do according to all that is written in it. For then you will make your way prosperous, and then you will have good success.
(Joshua 1:8)

Follow Where He Leads

Brother, sister, mother or father—follow the Lord's leading. He is ahead of you. Give him thanks even before he comes through, bringing all things together in your favor.

Reflect after a long struggle. Travel if you want. Explore. Find yourself. But in doing so, do it with him and not without. For without Him, life is dangerous and makes no sense. Engage your sense of responsibility.

Remember that sometimes the Lord takes long to give us something because he wants to protect us. Think this through quietly. Was there a response that took a while to come through? Consider why.

You were born for a purpose. In the womb, He designed you special. Seek to find out what He wants from you. Pray always and He will guide and show you the way. Always do the right thing even when no one is looking.

My prayer is that this will be your guide through today, tomorrow, and always.

Connect the Dots

Doesn't everything work through God, no matter how small? The food we eat, the friends we keep, the goals we make, the careers we choose, our spouses, and other relationships? Doesn't everything line up with God?

Personally, there was a time when I was waiting on God 's direction. My mind was alert to whatever came my way. A colleague shared some real life-changing news with me. As I reflected, I realized that the Lord had lined up everything in that space for her.

So I shared my gleanings. Her response, "you don't have to make everything so spiritual." She was a believer, so I gasped at her reaction. Her assumption was that I was being a little 'preachy.' Convicted, she later apologized.

It is particularly important to look back on our lives and connect the dots because no matter how small, everything lines up when we are in the will of the Lord. Personally, I do not want anything unless it is lined up with the Lord's leading. I had learnt many lessons over the years when I went off course. Then later, I realized that I was not in his will and everything was a waste of time.

So now I just want to do everything according to God's will. At times I will step back, examine, reflect, and connect the dots. This happened; that happened, and they are all lined up on the path that he had planned for me all along. How can you not praise God? How can you not?

Today, look back on your journey. Connect the dots. You will be surprised at what you discover.

My soul glorifies the Lord and my spirit rejoices in God my Savior. (Luke 1:46-47)

Open my Eyes

Open my eyes that I may see;

Open my ears that I may hear.

Open my lips that I may speak your beauty enthralled.

Open my hands that I may give;

My nose that I may receive your sweet-smelling savor.

Open my eyes Lord, please open my eyes.

Open my eyes, that I may behold wondrous things out of your law. (Psalm 119:18)

PSALM 143

Lord, hear my prayer,
listen to my cry for mercy;
in your faithfulness and righteousness
come to my relief.
Do not bring your servant into judgment,
for no one living is righteous before you.
The enemy pursues me,
he crushes me to the ground;
he makes me dwell in the darkness
like those long dead.
So my spirit grows faint within me;
my heart within me is dismayed.
I remember the days of long ago;
I meditate on all your works
and consider what your hands have done.
I spread out my hands to you;
I thirst for you like a parched land.

Answer me quickly, Lord;
my spirit fails.
Do not hide your face from me
or I will be like those who go down to the pit.
Let the morning bring me word of your unfailing love,
for I have put my trust in you.
Show me the way I should go,
for to you I entrust my life.
Rescue me from my enemies, Lord,
for I hide myself in you.
Teach me to do your will,
for you are my God;
may your good Spirit
lead me on level ground.

For your name's sake, Lord, preserve my life;
in your righteousness, bring me out of trouble.
In your unfailing love, silence my enemies;
destroy all my foes,
for I am your servant.

WORRIED

I See Walls

I see walls on every side of me.
Dark walls.
Brick walls.
Walls that seem to be made of steel and the toughest stone.
I cannot see my way through.
I am so overwhelmed.

But then, I am comforted in the knowledge that you Lord
can see for me.
As I hold onto you, you embrace me and hold me firm,
You comfort me with the words,
All will be well, and everything is going to be alright.

But Still my heart longs for those days when I do not have
to worry.
Lord, you are in control and I long for your quiet peace.
A peace that passes all understanding.
Unto you I lift up my praise.
My heart yearns for you in a dry and thirsty land.

For with Christ in the vessel I know I can smile at the storm

I will build you up again nation of Israel, you will be rebuilt. Once again you will plant vineyards on the hills of Samaria. Farmers will plant them. They will enjoy the fruit.

(Jeremiah 31:4-5)

I Have Been There

I have been there. When the issues of life overwhelm, I have been there. I have contemplated giving up when the bills pile up so high and the shame and disgrace threaten. I have contemplated all manner of actions to resolve these issues. Yes, I have been there.

But through it all, God sustained me. I am not there yet but where I am is in that safe place where like Abraham, I have the faith, hope and the assurance that my God takes care of all my needs. He is there when it all seems hopeless. But like Abraham, David, Job, Joseph, Moses, and the Israelites, He always comes through.

Today, spend time in his presence, for he is our deliverer.

The righteous cry out, and the Lord hears them; he delivers them from all their troubles.

(Psalm 34:17

The Thing About Depression and Suicide

When all seems hopeless

My friend deals with fatalities every day. She shared an incident of a woman whose car was severely damaged when it crashed into a Guard rail. The woman reported that she was trying to commit suicide. She survived.

On the other hand, my friend's hubby, who is in law enforcement, shared reports about a man who after investigation, authorities discovered it was attempted suicide. He succumbed to his injuries and died.

A Pastor in his message shared statistics of the number of police officers who committed suicide mid-2019 in New York, and it was an unbelievable rate of 24 percent.

I share this to ask prayers for those who smile or laugh out loud with us outwardly but deep down inside are hurting or depressed due to finances, job loss, relationships, or for one reason or another. Comedian Robin Williams is an example. Anthony Bourdain, celebrity author and travel documentarian is another. Not to mention the silent ones who go crazy with mass shootings of the innocent. All suicides. Sad indeed.

Let us not live in a vacuum. Look around. Consider the quiet signals of friends and loved ones. Signs can be seen from individuals who experience excessive sadness or moodiness, hopelessness, sleep problems, sudden calmness, withdrawal, change in personality or appearance, dangerous or self-harmful behavior, recent trauma, making preparations, threatening suicide and more.

If you are among the depressed, please seek help. Using wisdom, if you recognize the signs in a friend, relative, or co-worker, don't wait. Do something. Get the person the professional help they need. Usually, they cannot think clearly.

Yet be comforted and know that when all seems helpless, pray. While you are praying, pray even more. Prayer changes things. There is no doubt about that. Let us together do what we can in our small corner. But above all, keep the faith.

For God has not given us a spirit of fear, but of power and of love and of a sound mind.
(2 Timothy 1:7)

Live One Day at a Time

It is funny how many of us worry about the future. At times some pass away and are not even around to enjoy what they worried about. My sister had cancer and worried about leaving her kids. But because she knew she would not be around much longer after fighting the dreaded disease for over 12 years, she decided to put things in place for them to survive and thrive after she passed.

Some of us worry about tomorrow—what we are going to eat, what we will drink, and more. Yet when tomorrow becomes today, we find that we have enough for the day—often even more than enough. We are not satisfied with what we have. We want steak when mere chicken will do. We want a mansion when a small condo will do. We want vacations to share on social media and gain likes and followers when a quiet space will give our hearts peace.

May we become satisfied with the present. May we be satisfied with God's deserving provisions now. May we be comforted like Joseph who accomplished his will in prison and rose from the depths of the dark hole of false accusers to the heights of ruling a nation during its most severe time of need.

Lord, when we are weak, make us strong.

Who of you by worrying can add a single hour to your life? Since you cannot do this very little thing, why do you worry about the rest? (Luke 12:25-26)

The Touch

The touch. The son. The change. The effect.

You cannot study the son without being changed. Saul did. He spent most of his waking hours studying how to capture and persecute believers. But be assured that time spent in the word, time spent studying the son, you will be affected. Your life will change. Saul did and became Paul.

Do you have a problem that needs to be solved? Are you sad, depressed, and cannot find the will to go on? Spend time in the word and you are sure to find the cure, the remedy for your situation.

Be blessed.

*For as the rain and the snow come down from heaven
and do not return there but water the earth, making it
bring forth and sprout, giving seed to the sower and
bread to the eater, so shall my word be that goes out
from my mouth; it shall not return to me empty, but it
shall accomplish that which I purpose, and shall
succeed in the thing for which I sent it.*
(Isaiah 55:10-11)

Miraculous Miracle

A miracle is defined as *"something so difficult that only God can do it."* Therefore, as many examples recorded, Abraham had Isaac at 100 years old; the Lord delivered his people from exile; a virgin gave birth to a savior.

So, do not worry. The Lord is working things out for you, according to his will. Simply trust him, have faith, and continue to believe that what he says he will do. In time your plans will come through.

Remember, nothing is too hard for the Lord.

The Lord said to Abraham "is anything too hard for The Lord? (Genesis 18:14.)

PSALM 116

I love the Lord, for he heard my voice;
he heard my cry for mercy.
Because he turned his ear to me,
I will call on him as long as I live.

The cords of death entangled me,
the anguish of the grave came over me;
I was overcome by distress and sorrow.
Then I called on the name of the Lord:
"Lord, save me!"

The Lord is gracious and righteous;
our God is full of compassion.
The Lord protects the unwary;
when I was brought low, he saved me.

Return to your rest, my soul,
for the Lord has been good to you.

For you, Lord, have delivered me from death,
my eyes from tears,
my feet from stumbling,
that I may walk before the Lord
in the land of the living.

I trusted in the Lord when I said,
"I am greatly afflicted";
in my alarm I said,
"Everyone is a liar."

What shall I return to the Lord
for all his goodness to me?

I will lift up the cup of salvation
and call on the name of the Lord.
I will fulfill my vows to the Lord
in the presence of all his people.

Precious in the sight of the Lord
is the death of his faithful servants.
Truly I am your servant, Lord;
I serve you just as my mother did;
you have freed me from my chains.

I will sacrifice a thank offering to you
and call on the name of the Lord.
I will fulfill my vows to the Lord
in the presence of all his people,
in the courts of the house of the Lord—
in your midst, Jerusalem.

Praise the Lord.

ENCOURAGEMENT FOR THE SICK, NEEDY AND BEREAVED

Life's Curved Balls

Sometimes life throws us curved balls. We have no choice but to catch it, run with it, and ride the waves until it passes. It is what we do with it when it comes our way that counts.

Renowned Speaker Nick Vujicic, the limbless man, has inspired millions worldwide. He was born without arms and legs. He was depressed early in life but found the strength to survive, thrive and now uses his God-given gift to do great things. Who would ever have thought he would make such a difference? But with God, all things are possible.

So when the nuances of life hit us like a ton of bricks, it does not matter how subtly it rears its ugly head; hold strong. Keep going because only then will we be able to get back up to achieve what the Lord has laid on our heart to do.

*But now be strong, Zerubbabel,' declares the Lord.
'Be strong, Joshua son of Jozadak, the high priest. Be
strong, all you people of the land,' declares the Lord,
'and work. For I am with you,' declares the Lord
Almighty. (Haggai 2:4)*

I Hate my Life

"I hate my life. I hate my life. I hate my life." That was the chant I heard as I approached her. Why would anyone say that? Such a negative thought.

She had lost her husband. Her job. Her house. Her children. Her sense of independence. She felt she had nothing to live for. Beautiful. Smart. Educated professional she was, life had handed her troubles and turmoil over the last few years. In despair, she thought she could never overcome her life's tumultuous storms. What were the right words to comfort her?

There is hope. Yes, there is hope in Christ. You are strong and you will survive. The tide will change, so pray and keep going. With God's help, guidance, and support, you will find comfort in his safe arms.

I sought the Lord, and he answered me and delivered me from all my fears. (Psalm 34:4)

God Knows What Is In Your Heart

A few years ago, I lost my mom after she suffered a massive stroke after the sudden death of my stepfather. The day after my mom's passing, my brother died tragically. This happened in the space of 24 hours. Naturally, it was a lot to digest. I felt numb.

A friend gave me a sympathy card to encourage me in my time of need. The words comforted me during that time. I have kept it as a reminder whenever the going gets tough. I share these words in the hopes that you, too, may be encouraged in your time of need.

God knows what's in your heart and what you
need before you ask
Even when you don't know for sure, God knows
because he knows you
He knows the outcome of every situation
and he is guiding you
Even when you might feel that you have lost your way.
He knows how much you can bear, and he will give you
strength and fill you with his grace and blessings as he
walks with you every step of the way

~Unknown

*When you pass through the waters, I will be with you;
and through the rivers, they shall not overwhelm you;
when you walk through fire you shall not be burned,
and the flame shall not consume you. (Isiah 43:2)*

Everything Is Beautiful In It's Time

Everything is beautiful in its time. This is one of my most meaningful scripture verses. Once I was reflecting on a past experience and this verse came to me. Everything is beautiful in its time. Everything serves a purpose. Let us not regret our life experiences. The good, bad, the turmoil and triumphs all serve a purpose. For that purpose, we should give thanks.

Pray. Seek the Lord's help. Ask for his wisdom in guiding you to understand and put together all that is happening to you. But know that you will never be able to understand everything. For some things, we will never get the answers. But know that everything is beautiful. The Bible said it. Believe it.

For everything there is a season, a time for every activity under heaven. A time to be born and a time to die. A time to plant and a time to harvest. A time to kill and a time to heal. A time to tear down and a time to build up. A time to cry and a time to laugh. A time to grieve and a time to dance. A time to scatter stones and a time to gather stones. A time to embrace and a time to turn away. A time to search and a time to quit searching. A time to keep and a time to throw away. A time to tear and a time to mend. A time to be quiet and a time to speak. A time to love and a time to hate. A time for war and a time for peace.
(Ecclesiastes 3:1-8)

PSALM 23

The Lord is my shepherd, I lack nothing.
He makes me lie down in green pastures,
he leads me beside quiet waters,
he refreshes my soul.
He guides me along the right paths
for his name's sake.
Even though I walk
through the darkest valley,[a]
I will fear no evil,
for you are with me;
your rod and your staff,
they comfort me.

You prepare a table before me
in the presence of my enemies.
You anoint my head with oil;
my cup overflows.
Surely your goodness and love will follow me
all the days of my life,
and I will dwell in the house of the Lord
forever.

HAVE FAITH. TRUST HIM

When God Says No

How many times have you asked the Lord for something and he said no? No doubt, there are many times. Personally, as a child, my dream was always to become a nurse as I love taking care of others. For some reason, my path turned, and I ended up in banking which (through my responsibilities), stimulated my appetite for the Human Resource function. I transitioned into pharmaceuticals, then more direct healthcare, managing several medical clinics.

As I reflect, the Lord's purpose was to place me in an area where I was more able to affect patient care. This was initially through pharmaceuticals and later clinical care through managing the Administrator role of other healthcare professionals.

On the other hand, cancer took my mom, grandmother, and sister from our family despite our prayers for healing. Though I miss them terribly, his response was to provide them with spiritual healing from the wear and tear on their bodies. I could not be selfish in wanting them around me much longer.

So remember, sometimes God says yes. Other times he says no. The important thing we can do is to trust him. His plan is always best for you. Take some time to reflect on the path he has taken you through. He has given you the Green Light.

*But he said to me, "My grace is sufficient for you, for
my power is made perfect in weakness.
(2 Corinthians 12:9)*

Gone in a Flash

A report tells of a 40-year-old woman whose fear led her to the bank. She withdrew thousands of dollars from her account. Her intent—to keep it safe at home. Unfortunately, eyes penetrated her actions and snatched her life's savings just as she drove into her gated community. Her rainy-day saving was taken away, just like that—in a flash. Authorities searched, but to no avail. She wanted to protect what was hers safely at home to use during the pandemic rainy days. That day became a lightning flash ripping through her very soul—Gone in-a-flash.

It is sad—lots of pain and sorrow these days. In one sweep, a virus instilled fear affecting worldwide travel, vacation, stock market, business, job interviews, entertainment, relationships, behaviors, mental capacities and more.

But rest assured, it will pass. There is no surprise with God. The surprise is for us. He has got things under his control. Let us together trust him.

Do not store up for yourselves treasures on earth, where moths and vermin destroy, and where thieves break in and steal. 20 But store up for yourselves treasures in heaven, where moths and vermin do not destroy, and where thieves do not break in and steal. 21 For where your treasure is, there your heart will be also (Matthew 6:19-21)

When Things Converge

Liliana awoke with a start. She is going to do it! She grabbed the phone and courageously spoke with her former part-time boss, John. For months she thought about her internship but was paranoid that she would be turned down.

This time luck was on her side! A past associate and colleague recently connected with John for an opportunity, but he did not have the time to assist. He had promised that he would think about it. Now here was his chance. Liliana had all the time in the world to dedicate to the project for a full year of internship!

Amazing! Totally supernatural! When faith works, everything converges. What are you afraid of? Go ahead, pray. Then do it even if you are afraid. You never know; the Lord may allow things to converge with another person's dream.

*If any of you lacks wisdom, let him ask God, who
gives generously to all without reproach, and it will
be given him. But let him ask in faith, with no
doubting, for the one who doubts is like a wave of the
sea that is driven and tossed by the wind.*
(James 1:5-6)

Even If

Stay true to yourself, but always be open to learn. Even if....

God desires that we cling to Him—even if our loved one is not healed, even if we lose our job, even if we are persecuted. Sometimes God rescues us from danger in this life, and sometimes He does not. But the truth we can hold firmly is this: "The God we serve is able, loves us and is with us in every fiery trial. c. (Extract from our Daily Bread)

Am I a God at hand, declares the Lord, and not a God far away? Can a man hide himself in secret places so that I cannot see him? declares the Lord. Do I not fill heaven and earth? declares the Lord. (Jeremiah 23:23-24)

The Rainy Day

The rainy day is here. The day that most people save for. The worldwide pandemic brought it right to our shores. Many have fallen sick. Some have lost loved ones. Others lost jobs, career, health and now, for the most part, live in fear. Fear of being touched—in error, on purpose or even worse, being looked at directly. Six feet apart is the social distance. Yes, the rainy day is here.

Dollars falling. Nah, not the government's stimulus check during the pandemic. It was the news report that a restaurant decorated its walls with dollars. Yes, you heard it right. They decorated the walls with dollars! There was a story behind it. The details were sketchy, but one partner had encouraged the other that it might come in handy one-rainy-day. Now with the Corona virus worldwide scare, the day finally came. They used the money to help pay their workers and assist those in the community who needed a hot meal during the pandemic. So yes, the rainy day came.

In all of what happened, be assured that one thing remains forever—God. He never changes. Trust Him.

So do not fear, for I am with you; do not be dismayed, for I am your God. I will strengthen you and help you; I will uphold you with my righteous right hand. (Isaiah 41:10)

Closed Doors

Closed doors offer many opportunities for us to learn. Often, we are disappointed with delays as we seek the Lord's help in prayer to meet the needs and desires of our heart. May we gain the strength to wait to follow His lead. Dr. Charles Stanley encouraged that God can use our desires to teach us his ways. The Lord does it to mold us into his image; to prevent mistakes; to redirect our walk with him; to test our faith; to build perseverance as well as to buy us time.

At times, we fail to learn because of our impatience. Then later, we find that we were not ready for the opportunity. So today, I encourage you to remember that God's ways are not our ways, but he knows best. I encourage you to always trust him and seek his guidance.

Rejoice in hope, be patient in tribulation, be constant in prayer. (Romans 12:12)

A New Heart

Sophia was sick for what seemed like eons. Finally, doctors told her she would not survive unless she received a new heart. She began praying and on the final day of the year, she was told that they had found her a new heart. But finding a new heart for her meant someone else had to die.

I thought about Denzel Washington's movie—John Q. The story surrounded a young boy that needed a heart transplant, but he was 'not on the list' because his family could not cover the cost for the many procedures that came along with it. His father (Denzel) took drastic actions that ended up with him jailed but his son received a new heart and survived. But someone had to die.

In like manner, Jesus died so that we could live. He paid the ultimate price because he loved us so much. Our decisions and actions may not be as drastic as those mentioned. But the Lord wants to give us all a new heart. Whether we are in good health, sick, hurting or in love, the heart that the Lord gives us replaces any condition our own hearts are in. Let us accept his love through accepting his irreplaceable gift of a new heart.

Remember God's ways are not our ways.

For still the vision awaits its appointed time; it hastens to the end—it will not lie. If it seems slow, wait for it; it will surely come; it will not delay.
(Habakkuk 2:3)

What if I Can't Do It?

My daughter's 6-year-old said to me after his ceremony, "what if I can't do first—grade work?" I smiled, then replied, "You can. You will. They will teach you." But what if I do not listen? Again, I smiled.

Aren't we all like that little 6-year-old? The world often seems bigger than us. We receive the new job, the new position, the contract, the opportunity, the leadership role, the marriage proposal, and the pregnancy news. We are thrilled! Over-joyed! But soon, as we reflect, we begin to ponder… "can I do it?"

My response is always—YES! Yes, you can do it! Often with new ventures or experiences, our goals seem insurmountable, especially from a distance when we cannot see our way. We falter. We fuss. We are afraid. These are all very normal but like I have always said, do not let fear stop you. Pray. Make that bold move. Do it in Portions. Do it even when you are afraid. Who knows? You may be surprised what the Lord can do through you.

When You Cannot See, Trust Him

Fear gripped me. A 2-hour journey turned into three as clouds stormed. The foggy skies were comfortless. Visibility was almost naught as the storm pounded. Headlights shone brightly as my hands tightly gripped the car's steering wheel. My commute slowed as my heart panicked. I began to pray. Then prayed louder with a shout and asked, "what's happening Lord?" Suddenly the rain slowed. Though it did not stop, I began to see. Alone, I praised as never before. Highway praise!

The Fog

Experiencing a season of storm in your life? Hold firmly onto our heavenly father. Pray without ceasing. When you cannot see what lies ahead, trust him. He will work things out for your good.

Blessings overflow

Too Helpful. Is That Even Possible?

"Don't help me." That was her cry each time I tried to assist. Too helpful. Is that even possible? Well, my hairdresser thinks so. I often help when she is doing my hair. Hold my head up when she wants it down. Hold it down, turn to the side, this way or that. All going against her desire and affecting the progress she was trying to make. So she always says, "Shell, please don't help me."

Isn't it the same with our Heavenly Father? Sometimes we step in to help but do more harm than good. Often, we end up in a different direction which may last anywhere from a short to a long time. It all depends on when we learn or get back on track.

Today, let us let go and let God have His way in our life.

I waited patiently for the Lord; he inclined to me and heard my cry. (Psalm 40:1)

God Will Make A Way

Years ago, when I was contemplating a big life change, I walked into a bookstore and asked the Lord to guide me. After about an hour browsing around, I saw the book "God will make a way." The title alone spoke to me. Since then, every now and again, I return to the title for encouragement as I wait expectantly on the Lord.

Wait on the Lord; He will come through.

Blessings overflow.

PSALM 71

In you, Lord, I have taken refuge;
let me never be put to shame.
In your righteousness, rescue me and deliver me;
turn your ear to me and save me.
Be my rock of refuge,
to which I can always go;
give the command to save me,
for you are my rock and my fortress.
Deliver me, my God, from the hand of the wicked,
from the grasp of those who are evil and cruel.

For you have been my hope, Sovereign Lord,
my confidence since my youth.
From birth I have relied on you;
you brought me forth from my mother's womb.
I will ever praise you.
I have become a sign to many;
you are my strong refuge.
My mouth is filled with your praise,
declaring your splendor all day long.

Do not cast me away when I am old;
do not forsake me when my strength is gone.
For my enemies speak against me;
those who wait to kill me conspire together.
They say, "God has forsaken him;
pursue him and seize him,
for no one will rescue him."
Do not be far from me, my God;
come quickly, God, to help me.
May my accusers perish in shame;
may those who want to harm me
be covered with scorn and disgrace.

As for me, I will always have hope;
I will praise you more and more.

My mouth will tell of your righteous deeds,
of your saving acts all day long—
though I know not how to relate them all.
I will come and proclaim your mighty acts, Sovereign Lord;
I will proclaim your righteous deeds, yours alone.
Since my youth, God, you have taught me,
and to this day I declare your marvelous deeds.
Even when I am old and gray,
do not forsake me, my God,
till I declare your power to the next generation,
your mighty acts to all who are to come.

Your righteousness, God, reaches to the heavens,
you who have done great things.
Who is like you, God?
Though you have made me see troubles,
many and bitter,
you will restore my life again;
from the depths of the earth
you will again bring me up.
You will increase my honor
and comfort me once more.

I will praise you with the harp
for your faithfulness, my God;
I will sing praise to you with the lyre,
Holy One of Israel.
My lips will shout for joy
when I sing praise to you—
I whom you have delivered.
My tongue will tell of your righteous acts
all day long,
for those who wanted to harm me
have been put to shame and confusion.

WHEN ENEMIES STRIKE

I Don't Forgive Him

"I don't forgive him. I don't forgive the justice system. I believe it failed me." This retort after a drunk driver recklessly crashed and hit a bystander. A man, a father, a husband, a friend who was innocently standing nearby.

Years later, after the court ruling, his surviving wife was angry when the guilty driver was released with a few simple charges for his actions. It is hard. Indeed it is very hard to accept. It is like the drunk driver walked away with a slap on the wrist while his family was forced to go on and live life without him.

Forgive? Why? Is it necessary to forgive under such circumstances? Did the court 'fail' the family? Could the husband and father have been standing somewhere else on that fateful day? So many questions. All remain unanswered.

But why forgive? Because it frees. Yes, it does. But only if you allow it. Personally, my own brother suffered such fate, leaving his son to grow up without him. But let us allow God to do His thing—and if He doesn't (as far as the naked eye can see), you can be assured that we are all held accountable for our actions in one way or another.

Be comforted. Know that healing takes time, and the Lord will provide the strength.

Do not repay anyone evil for evil. Be careful to do what is right in the eyes of everyone. If it is possible, as far as it depends on you, live at peace with everyone. Do not take revenge, my dear friends, but leave room for God's wrath, for it is written: It is mine to avenge, I will repay, says the Lord (Romans 12:17-19)

Enemy Hungry? Feed Him

Cunningham was going through hell at work. His co-worker did everything in his power to undermine his work. Despite his efforts to reveal the dark actions of his co-worker, management was not convinced. Finally, it got so bad that Cunningham went home and asked his family to pray deeply for him.

On arrival at work the next day, he was greeted with the news that his co-worker had resigned. What? He was confused. This was a manager who had been with the company for almost two decades. He rushed to the phone to share the news with his family. Alleluia! Since then, Cunningham has taken any issue he experienced directly to the Lord.

Your enemy hungry? Feed him. Never take matters into your own hands without consulting the Lord for he has said, vengeance is mine, I will repay.

*If your enemy is hungry, feed him. If he is thirsty,
give him something to drink. In doing this, you will
heap burning coals on his head. Do not be overcome
by evil but overcome evil with good.*
(Romans 12:20-21)

PSALM 27

The Lord is my light and my salvation—
whom shall I fear?
The Lord is the stronghold of my life—
of whom shall I be afraid?

When the wicked advance against me
to devour[a] me,
it is my enemies and my foes
who will stumble and fall.
Though an army besiege me,
my heart will not fear;
though war break out against me,
even then I will be confident.

One thing I ask from the Lord,
this only do I seek:
that I may dwell in the house of the Lord
all the days of my life,
to gaze on the beauty of the Lord
and to seek him in his temple.
For in the day of trouble
he will keep me safe in his dwelling;
he will hide me in the shelter of his sacred tent
and set me high upon a rock.

Then my head will be exalted
above the enemies who surround me;
at his sacred tent I will sacrifice with shouts of joy;
I will sing and make music to the Lord.

Hear my voice when I call, Lord;
be merciful to me and answer me.

My heart says of you, "Seek his face!"
Your face, Lord, I will seek.
Do not hide your face from me,
do not turn your servant away in anger;
you have been my helper.
Do not reject me or forsake me,
God my Savior.
Though my father and mother forsake me,
the Lord will receive me.
Teach me your way, Lord;
lead me in a straight path
because of my oppressors.
Do not turn me over to the desire of my foes,
for false witnesses rise up against me,
spouting malicious accusations.

I remain confident of this:
I will see the goodness of the Lord
in the land of the living.
Wait for the Lord;
be strong and take heart
and wait for the Lord.

PRAY

I Didn't Know What Else to Do

"I did not know what else to do. So I prayed with everyone." That was the comment from an eyewitness to a tragic accident when two teenagers who were about to graduate high school lost their lives. This happened while they were driving home late one night. They were just five minutes away from home when the tragedy occurred.

The eyewitness said she did not know what to do to help comfort the surviving teenagers, who were driving behind in another car, so she 'resorted' to prayer.

Aren't we all like that? It is when we have exhausted all other options that we decide to pray. We have it skewed. Lord help us remember to give prayer precedence in our lives and not be the last resort.

And this is the confidence that we have toward him, that if we ask anything according to his will he hears us. And if we know that he hears us in whatever we ask, we know that we have the requests that we have asked of him. (1 John 5:14-15)

In The Midst of life's Busyness

Amidst life's busyness, let us not forget to pray—to have time with the Lord. Personally, sometimes I feel far from Him and that is when He nudges me quietly. Then I return to him in quiet rest.

Thank you, Lord, for not giving up on us and for granting us your peace.

Likewise the Spirit helps us in our weakness. For we do not know what to pray for as we ought, but the Spirit himself intercedes for us with groanings too deep for words. And he who searches hearts knows what is the mind of the Spirit, because the Spirit intercedes for the saints according to the will of God. (Romans 8:26-27)

Deprived of Life's Simple Things

Deprived. Deprived of sleep. Deprived of food, shelter, love, or the ability to satisfy life's basic needs can create longings so deep that words can hardly describe. I spent a week traveling by plane, train, bus, taxicabs, and on foot across the nation's capital, Washington DC. Severe weather conditions created havoc causing flight cancellations, delays, hunger, and deprivation of simple necessities.

Enter a positive mental attitude. Delays provided the opportunity to read, people-watch, and smile at life's little things. Things that commonly get lost when things are going right.

I walked away, being thankful for life's setback. I did not like the delays and at times, got quite annoyed. But deprivation provided opportunities for resilience, creativity, and most of all, to bask in the knowledge that God uses life's simple things to get us closer to him.

What you have learned and received and heard and seen in me—practice these things, and the God of peace will be with you. (Philippians 4:5)

Before We Ask

Ever had that experience where the Lord seems to respond while you are on your knees? While you're praying? Just as you were about to ask. It leaves us astonished, doesn't it? He sends a neighbor, a stranger, a friend with his answer.

Today, let us remember he sees, hears, knows, comforts, and responds to us. Let us do our part to ask. Be confident that through prayer and supplication, he meets our needs.

When he answers, let's not forget to say Thanks.

Blessings overflow.

Before they call, I will answer; while they are still speaking, I will hear. (Isiah 54:24)

My Prayer for You

My darling. My daughter. My beloved.
My prayer for you is:

That the Lord will be with you always.
That he will be your guide.
That he will grant you success in all that you do.
That he will grant you peace.
That he will grant you great friends to uplift you.

That he will take care of the family
that he has planned for you.
That he will lead you to them.
That he will grant you the desires of your heart.
That he will be with you when you are alone.

That your cup will overflow with joy and gladness.
That he will bring you his quiet peace in that safe place as
he comforts you in his everlasting arms.

Whatever brings you joy, think on those things.

Finally, brothers, whatever is true, whatever is honorable, whatever is just, whatever is pure, whatever is lovely, whatever is commendable, if there is any excellence, if there is anything worthy of praise, think about these things. (Philippians 4:8)

Prayer is Not a Checklist

Children love to play. They will play up to the very last minute before going to bed with the threat of being tired in the mornings before school. One Sunday night, as my daughter's kids played, they turned to me and I suggested that we just pray because I am tired and will be going to sleep early without waiting on them.

Together they exclaimed, "Granshell prayer is not just a checklist." Guilty, I laughed because I had taught them that. Though there is value in it, I never taught them the rhetorical children's prayer—now I lay me down to sleep, I pray the Lord my soul to keep. I taught them to always give thanks for food and shelter. To pray for the homeless, their parents, grandparents, and extended family.

Since then, they understand and pray even when they want something like a puppy, birthday, Christmas gifts and more. May we as adults display the spirit of prayer to our youths so they know that prayer is not seen as a checklist.

Take Five minutes to pray each day. Commit your thoughts and dreams to the one most high. He will see you through your doubts and fears.

Pray. It works.

If Only They Knew

Ever thought of writing a letter to God? Many have. Some have mailed it. Our Daily Bread shared reports of thousands of letters being mailed to Jerusalem by individuals who seek the lord's help. They ask for health, wealth, child, and more. If only they knew.

If only they knew that the very act of writing a letter to God is praying to him. The very act of writing is seeking his intervention. The very act of writing is exactly what is needed for our Lord, the problem-solver, to work in our lives. The very act of writing is spending time in his presence to find the comfort needed for trying times.

Today do not hesitate to spend time in his presence. Talk. Write. Sing. Do whatever works for you. He will intervene, comfort, and answer your prayer.

Blessings overflow.

Therefore I tell you, whatever you ask in prayer,
believe that you have received it, and it will be yours.
(Mark 11:24)

Life is a Matter of Choices

The choices we make, we should first consider where they will lead. Is it marriage, love, children, new job, college, new contract, new house? Always contemplate the future. Where will your choice lead you?

It is simple. Pray. Consider carefully. Have faith and then make your decision based on the spirit's leading.

Trust him.

PSALM 37

Do not fret because of those who are evil
or be envious of those who do wrong;
for like the grass they will soon wither,
like green plants they will soon die away.

Trust in the Lord and do good;
dwell in the land and enjoy safe pasture.
Take delight in the Lord,
and he will give you the desires of your heart.

Commit your way to the Lord;
trust in him and he will do this:
He will make your righteous reward shine like the dawn,
your vindication like the noonday sun.

Be still before the Lord
and wait patiently for him;
do not fret when people succeed in their ways,
when they carry out their wicked schemes.

Refrain from anger and turn from wrath;
do not fret—it leads only to evil.
For those who are evil will be destroyed,
but those who hope in the Lord will inherit the land.

A little while, and the wicked will be no more;
though you look for them, they will not be found.
But the meek will inherit the land
and enjoy peace and prosperity.

The wicked plot against the righteous
and gnash their teeth at them;
but the Lord laughs at the wicked,
for he knows their day is coming.

The wicked draw the sword
and bend the bow
to bring down the poor and needy,
to slay those whose ways are upright.
But their swords will pierce their own hearts,
and their bows will be broken.

Better the little that the righteous have
than the wealth of many wicked;
for the power of the wicked will be broken,
but the Lord upholds the righteous.

The blameless spend their days under the Lord's care,
and their inheritance will endure forever.
In times of disaster they will not wither;
in days of famine they will enjoy plenty.

But the wicked will perish:
Though the Lord's enemies are like the flowers of the field,
they will be consumed, they will go up in smoke.

The wicked borrow and do not repay,
but the righteous give generously;
those the Lord blesses will inherit the land,
but those he curses will be destroyed.

The Lord makes firm the steps
of the one who delights in him;

though he may stumble, he will not fall,
for the Lord upholds him with his hand.

I was young and now I am old,
yet I have never seen the righteous forsaken
or their children begging bread.
They are always generous and lend freely;
their children will be a blessing.[b]

Turn from evil and do good;
then you will dwell in the land forever.
For the Lord loves the just
and will not forsake his faithful ones.

Wrongdoers will be completely destroyed[c];
the offspring of the wicked will perish.
The righteous will inherit the land
and dwell in it forever.

The mouths of the righteous utter wisdom,
and their tongues speak what is just.
The law of their God is in their hearts;
their feet do not slip.

The wicked lie in wait for the righteous,
intent on putting them to death;
but the Lord will not leave them in the power of the wicked
or let them be condemned when brought to trial.

Hope in the Lord
and keep his way.
He will exalt you to inherit the land;
when the wicked are destroyed, you will see it.

I have seen a wicked and ruthless man
flourishing like a luxuriant native tree,
but he soon passed away and was no more;
though I looked for him, he could not be found.

Consider the blameless, observe the upright;
a future awaits those who seek peace.[d]
But all sinners will be destroyed;
there will be no future[e] for the wicked.

The salvation of the righteous comes from the Lord;
he is their stronghold in time of trouble.
The Lord helps them and delivers them;
he delivers them from the wicked and saves them,
because they take refuge in him.

WAIT ON THE LORD

Wondering What to Do
While Waiting On God?

Pondering what to do while waiting on God? Finding out the Lord's will? We all have. When we examine the past, we know that some grew impatient and did their own thing while others trusted and waited patiently. Let us look at a few examples of people who could not wait.

People Who Could Not Wait

Abraham and Sarah thought they were too old to achieve God's promises. They ended up outside his will after doing their own thing. To their surprise, when Abraham was almost a century (in his 90s), Sarah gave birth to a son accomplishing God's promises.

Mary and Martha gave up on the Lord's intervention to save their brother. He was too late. Lazarus had already died. But still, the promise was achieved, showcasing one of the greatest miracles of all time.

The Disciples in the Garden of Gethsemane fell asleep. Their bodies too tired to stay awake as instructed. Later they were to partake in one of history's legendary fate—the death of Christ.

Then there were the people who couldn't wait on Moses to return and built a tower going against God's plan. They succumbed to a life of misery.

People Who Waited

Now here are a few examples of people who waited. David's rise to the throne. Despite his many turmoils, he wrote many Psalms while he waited. Dive in. Read. Be encouraged during your own periods of waiting, depression, and delays.

Joseph suffered betrayal, harm, hurt, pain. He was even innocently thrown in prison. Yet was later elevated to lead a time of severe famine in Egypt.

Noah through turmoil, mocking and embarrassment, stayed true to the divine instructions. He built an ark and participated in an historical feat so we could have a second chance.

Oh, let us not forget Job, who lost his kids and his riches. As if that was not enough, he became increasingly sick. Yet, in the midst of it all, he refused to curse God and die. He recovered and was blessed with abundance more than before.

So if you are wondering what to do while waiting, these five things will help. First, simply pray. Second, read the word. Third, stay close to him. Fourth, listen for his response and fifth, praise him while you wait.

Above all else, trust God. His timing is always right.

*I waited patiently for the Lord; he inclined to me and
heard my cry. He drew me up from the pit of
destruction, out of the miry bog, and set my feet upon
a rock, making my steps secure. He put a new song in
my mouth, a song of praise to our God. Many will see
and fear and put their trust in the Lord.*
(Psalm 40:1-3)

Sometimes you will have to do it Afraid

Excited, yet terrified! But does it stop us? No! The excitement! The adrenalin rush pushes us forward despite our fears.

I did a sky-dive which was one of the most terrifying things in my life. I was scared that certain death faced me 14,000 ft. below if anything went wrong. But I did it anyway. I jumped and was able to share with my two girls that they can do anything they put their minds to.

Sometimes we must jump in-spite of our fears! Those difficult goals. Those glaring entrepreneurial feat that tends to freeze us as we face life's challenges. Our fears heighten because of what we foresee in the future if things go awry. But do not let anxiety retard your progress. Move forward and in faith, do what you must. You may even surprise yourself with delight at the amazing things you can accomplish once you step outside your comfort zone.

So go ahead, do it even when you are afraid. The Lord—he has got you.

The Lord is my rock, my fortress, and my deliverer.
(Psalm 18:2)

Living Your Life As A Mask

A new writer shared her Instagram name. It was nowhere close to her real name. I beckoned to her, smile in tow. "You do make it hard, don't you?" In haste, she quickly countered, "it's so my employer can't find me." I smiled.

How many of us are like that? We live our lives in compartments trying to separate our true selves from what those around us see publicly.

To hide. To be. It is a hard choice but sometimes you must hide in order 'to be.' I pray one day that you will be able to just—be. To reveal your true identity and just be the you that you want to be.

With God's help, you will find that sure solace.

When I am afraid, I put my trust in you. (Psalm 56:3)

Life's Uncertainties

Life's uncertainties at times leave us baffled–often as if in a maze with no way out. The unseen provides periods of confusion, apprehension, and fear. It seems we are running a Marathon–a race that never seems to end.

But it is at those times that our strength and character grow immeasurably. If we hold on and never give up, we discover things about ourselves we never knew existed. With renewed zeal we embrace our inner desires to go on. To achieve even more goals, dreams, and aspirations far beyond measure.

Today if you feel exhausted, take a break. Pray. Talk to the Lord. But whatever you do, do not ever give up. The light will break through at the end of the tunnel because the Lord sees, hears, and knows what you are going through.

Keep the faith.

*Command those who are rich in this present world
not to be arrogant nor to put their hope in wealth,
which is so uncertain, but to put their hope in God,
who richly provides us with everything for our
enjoyment. (1 Timothy 6:17)*

When All Is Nothing

You have a room that provide shelter, a sure place to sleep.
You have food on the table, a variety to eat.
You have a car that provides transport; ability to commute.
But all is for nothing, for that's a safe place for you.

You are at that place where all you have is grace.
You are down to your last resort and your last resort is the Lord explicitly.
It is as if you are at the bottom of the well with nowhere to turn.
If only you could look up and hold your safety firm.

Your head is held low as you feel sorry for yourself.
It is kept down so others won't see the conflicts that exist internally.
The dread that society has caused you to be.
Nothing, absolutely nothing is okay within.

A visionary in your past life, now you can hardly see.
Will you ever get back to the heights of self-confidence that you have been known to preach? Will life turn 360 so you can see what is for real?
You have never been an oppressor, but depressed and oppressed is all you seem to see.

May the Lord bring you back to those days of confidence and habitat that surely exists for real.

Be still before the Lord and wait patiently for him; fret not yourself over the one who prospers in his way, over the man who carries out evil devices. Refrain from anger and forsake wrath. Fret not yourself; it tends only to evil. For the evildoers shall be cut off, but those who wait for the Lord shall inherit the land. (Psalm 37:7-9)

PSALM 130

Out of the depths I cry to you, Lord;
Lord, hear my voice.
Let your ears be attentive
to my cry for mercy.

If you, Lord, kept a record of sins,
Lord, who could stand?
But with you there is forgiveness,
so that we can, with reverence, serve you.

I wait for the Lord, my whole being waits,
and in his word I put my hope.
I wait for the Lord
more than watchmen wait for the morning,
more than watchmen wait for the morning.

Israel, put your hope in the Lord,
for with the Lord is unfailing love
and with him is full redemption.
He himself will redeem Israel
from all their sins.

TIME ALONE WITH THE LORD

TIME FOR ME

Time for me Holy Spirit.

Time for me to praise your name.

Time to hear your Spirit's leading.

Time to read your holy word.

Time. Oh, time for me to be with you

Time to bask in your presence.

Time to seek your holy decadence.

Time to praise the one above me.

Time to sing hallelujah.

Time to shout your Spirit's name   .

Time. Oh, time for me.

Time to hide in your arms for comfort.

Time to seek your spirit's lead.

Time. Oh, time for me to be with you

*Immediately Jesus made the disciples get into the
boat and go on ahead of him to the other side, while
he dismissed the crowd. After he had dismissed them,
he went up on a mountainside by himself to pray.
(Matthew 14:22-23)*

He is My Peace

Emily and her husband went to Rehab to visit their grandfather—a retired senior Pastor. The staff searched everywhere, including the halls, dining area, rooms but could not find him. Frantic, they expanded their search outdoors and into the streets. He was later found sitting quietly under a tree in an excluded area reading the book, *GreenLight: When God Says Go.*

The family shared the news of the incident with a friend and that is when I knew that the book was a treasure for the sick and lonely. Through the inspired word, the Lord calms our soul as we go about our father's business.

And he said unto them, How is it that you sought me?
Did you not know that I must be about my Father's
business? (Luke 2:49)

The Rush for Time

"You have to drive around ma'am; we have a time-to-customer-service that we have to meet," drawled the drive-through window clerk.

Growing kids have appetites that sometimes seem never-ending. So auntie drove into Burger King during her commute with the kids. She ordered food for the boys amidst repeated requests, "will that be all ma'am?" With each question, she felt rushed. She wanted something herself but not one from fast food; she decided to ask for help when she got to the drive-through window. While paying for the kids' order, she asked whether she could get a sandwich. That is when she was told that she would have to join the line of traffic again to get another sandwich. What in the world? She thought she misunderstood, so she sought clarification. That is when she was told that the employees have a set-time-to-meet-each-order and she was affecting it. In disbelief, she again sought clarification. Several minutes later, the same response from the supervisor on duty. Out of consideration for the growing line of famished drivers waiting behind her, auntie drove away. Lose-lose situation for sure.

In another incident, the Fedex delivery guy tossed the package at the door. Without ringing the doorbell, he quickly made his getaway. This act repeatedly done over his six-hour route as he tried to meet his targeted goals. Oh, the haste to deliver packages door to door.

There are many more situations that can be shared about the new focus on meeting deadlines to the detriment of quality service. Dismantled packages. Incorrect orders. Broken pieces. All creates havoc for service departments. So goes the new trend in delivery, Uber-eats, and all. Compliance divisions pay thousands of dollars to dissatisfied customers in their attempt to correct terrible behaviors.

These situations caused me to think, where is God's private time with you? Amidst the hustle and bustle of life, where is His time with you? —The question to ponder in our now microwave society.

But when you pray, go into your room, and shut the door and pray to your Father who is in secret. And your Father who sees in secret will reward you openly. (Matthew 6:6)

Beneath the Shadows

In the cleft is my favorite place to be. This temporary space helps me hide from my infirmities, wants, needs, and desires.

Beneath the shadows, I lie in wait for the Lord's amazing answers. In between, He comforts, leads, and guides. As I wait (at times impatiently), He grants me peace and quiet solace. The pace, growth, love, and understanding are all he asks.

He is my peace. Allow him to be yours too.

When my glory passes by, I will put you in a cleft in the rock and cover you with my hand until I have passed by. (Exodus 33:22)

PSALM 46

God is our refuge and strength,
an ever-present help in trouble.
Therefore we will not fear, though the earth give way
and the mountains fall into the heart of the sea,
though its waters roar and foam
and the mountains quake with their surging.[c]

There is a river whose streams make glad the city of God,
the holy place where the Most High dwells.
God is within her, she will not fall;
God will help her at break of day.
Nations are in uproar, kingdoms fall;
he lifts his voice, the earth melts.

The Lord Almighty is with us;
the God of Jacob is our fortress.

Come and see what the Lord has done,
the desolations he has brought on the earth.
He makes wars cease
to the ends of the earth.
He breaks the bow and shatters the spear;
he burns the shields[d] with fire.
He says, "Be still, and know that I am God;
I will be exalted among the nations,
I will be exalted in the earth."

The Lord Almighty is with us;
the God of Jacob is our fortress.

BE THANKFUL

All Things Are Working for our Good

Lord, we thank you that all things are working together for our good.
We give you thanks for all you have done.
Lord, thank you for all that is happening in our lives right now.

We thank you for:
For making us strong when weakness is all we have, we thank you.
For Green Lights, we thank you
For mortgage and car payments, we thank you.
For the satisfactory purpose and the job or entrepreneur venture you provide, we thank you.

For the bills it will pay, we thank you.
For being able to give back to you and to help others, we thank you.
For the peace that only you can give and will continue to provide, we thank you.
For resilience, we thank.
For sustenance, when all we want to do is to give up, we thank you.
For manipulators and their conniving schemes that use to try to break us, but we are made stronger, we thank you.

For being our stronghold in times of trouble, we thank you.
For tears we shed as we hold on to you, we thank you.
For shelter, food, and clothing that you provide, and we so often take them for granted, we thank you.
For learning your purpose in all situations, we thank you.
For you never giving up on us, we thank you,

For taking care of our children and family as only you can when we are not physically present and you are the only one there, we thank you.

For spiritual growth, we thank you.
For the pillow that we lay our heads on at night, we thank you.
For not giving up on us when we falter and go astray, we thank you.
For using us to take care of the sick, we thank you.
For your never-ending love, we thank you.

In all things, we thank you. We thank you.
We forever thank you.

I will give thanks to the Lord because of his righteousness; I will sing the praises of the name of the Lord Most High. (Psalm 7:17)

Mistakes and Learnings

Giving thanks to God for life. Sometimes we do not know what to think when things go awry. When we get worried and think the worst, but while there is life, there is hope.

So do not dwell on past mistakes. Work on the issues with Christ as your leader and guide. Whether the mistake pertains to family or professional life, community, or church, it may be a challenge but be comforted in the knowledge that this too will pass.

Start today in prayer, taking things a step-at-time. One day-at-a-time. Often it gets harder before it gets easier. Remember, as bad as things are or will get—you can do all through Christ.

While there's life there's hope because our hope is in Christ alone.

Forget the former things; do not dwell on the past. See, I am doing a new thing. Now it springs up; do you not perceive it? I am making a way in the wilderness and streams in the wasteland.
(Isaiah 43:18-19)

Thy Word Have I Hid in My Heart

Thy word have I hid in my heart that I may be strong among those who try to restrain me.

Thy word have I hid in my heart that I may steadily rise above injustices.

Thy word have I hid in my heart that I may never let go despite the strain that heavily weighs me down.

Thy word have I hid in my heart that I may fight the good fight until my days are done.

Thy word have I hid in my heart that I may confidently stride to attain new heights of gain.

Thy word have I hid in my heart that I may persevere beyond the trials that intercepts me.

Thy word have I hid in my heart that I may show resilience to those arising; be it children, young adults or seniors with memories long gone, yet unforgettable

Thy word have I hid in my heart that I may not fall prey and sin against Thee.

Thy word have I hid in my heart that I may be strong because of Thee.

Thy word I have hid in my heart that I may not sin against thee. (Psalms 119:11)

The Gift

Christmas. It is my favorite time of year! Anyone who knows me can share that I say Merry Christmas all year round. For me, it is a time to give and give and give. It brings me joy to see the receivers bask in a well-thought-out gift to a recipient. But I am bad when it comes to receiving from others. Pride, I would say. Not to forget the silliness mixed within as I share this story that depicts the extent of my sphere.

One Christmas, my boss gave me a gift. It was an envelope. Being the sentimental person that I am, I tucked the envelope away to read later. I love reading and value words. Four months later, while going through some stuff on my nightstand, I discovered an envelope. Curious, I opened it wondering why—or if I had forgotten to open it. Sure enough, I had. When I opened it, there was a Christmas card that had a grand monetary gift in it. With a gasp, I immediately called and enquired the reason she had not asked if I had seen it. She just smiled.

It caused me to think. God gives us many valuable gifts packaged in different ways. But if we never open it, we will never receive the value he has in store for us. Why not open your gift today? Accept the value he has for you.

For it is by grace you have been saved, through faith, and this is not from yourselves, it is the gift of God. (Ephesians 2:8) Thanks be to God for His indescribable gift. (2 Corinthians 9:15)

Miracles

A Miracle is defined as something only God can do.

Today, may the Lord grant you miracles beyond your heart's desires. Amen.

*Jesus replied, "What is impossible with man is
possible with God"
(Luke 18:27)*

PSALM 100

Shout for joy to the Lord, all the earth.
Worship the Lord with gladness;
come before him with joyful songs.
Know that the Lord is God.
It is he who made us, and we are his[a];
we are his people, the sheep of his pasture.

Enter his gates with thanksgiving
and his courts with praise;
give thanks to him and praise his name.
For the Lord is good and his love endures forever;
his faithfulness continues through all generations.

ABOUT DR SHELLY CAMERON

Dr. Shelly Cameron is an Author of non-fiction books on Personal Growth and inspiration. She is an Organizational Leadership Specialist. Through her book Success Strategies of Immigrant Leaders, she revealed the results of a Phenomenological study conducted with Nova Southeastern University and published in the Journal of American Academy of Business Cambridge (JAABC) which explored the hidden secrets of successful leaders. She now connects it to those aspiring to achieve. Individuals are challenged to take that first step to accomplish their dreams, goals, and aspirations.

An award-winning Author, Speaker, and Coach, Dr. Cameron helps aspiring first-time authors write and publish their books. She holds Graduate degrees in Organizational Leadership, Health Administration, Human Resource Development and Business.

An avid believer in Prayer, Dr. Cameron has traveled as far as Kenya, East Africa on Missions to share her Passion for Prayer and its link to Personal Development. She holds firmly to the stance that All Things Are Possible with God.

When not writing Shelly enjoys wave-watching, movies, reading, and spending time with family.

Connect with Dr. Shelly

www.shellycameron.com

https://www.facebook.com/pg/DrShellyCameron/

https://twitter.com/drshellyc

https://www.instagram.com/drShellyC_Success/

Thanks for Reading!

If you loved the book and have a moment to spare,

I would appreciate a short review as this helps new readers find my books.

Follow me on Instagram, Twitter or Facebook

www.shellycameron.com

OTHER BOOKS BY
DR SHELLY CAMERON

The Leadership Challenge:
Caribbean American Leaders in the United States
Published in Journal of American Academy of Business
Cambridge (JAABC)

Success Strategies of Immigrant Leaders
in the United States

Your Career. Ditch It. Switch It

My Safe Place

GreenLight: When God Says Go
Also available as Audiobook

GreenLight Journal

101+ Empowering Quotes For New Entrepreneurs

Motivational Quotes To Boost Your Success

Success Strategies Workbook

Success Strategies of Caribbean American Leaders
in the United States